CONTROL

Letting Go of It to Get It

JASON TERPACK

CONTROL

LETTING GO OF IT TO GET IT

Jason Terpack
2019

Control

ISBN 978-0-578-59768-3

This book is lovingly dedicated to the women who helped to shape my life:

Stephenie-My Beautiful and Patient Wife

Lisa Blythe-My Loving Mother

Carolyn Goode-My favorite person ever - *my Nana*

Aloria Gurganus-My Church Youth Group Mother

Introduction

Social media addiction…

Question: Why are we constantly obsessed with checking our Facebook®, Twitter®, and Instagram®?

Answer: Because it gives us a sense of being in control. However, it is a false sense of control. It gives us the idea that by clicking "like" and by scrolling through to read the instant feeds of friends and strangers alike, we are somehow in control. BUT WE ARE NOT!

In reality, instead of being in control by controlling our smartphones or computers, these things are controlling us.

They're controlling our time.

They're controlling our energy.

They're controlling our emotions.

And the sad thing is-we're allowing them to. So what can we do to STOP IT?

WHY CONTROL?

Control. Why do people want to be in control?

Why do people overeat?

Why do people drink to forget?

Why do people do drugs?

Why are people workaholics?

Do you want to know why? Do you do some of these things and even wonder at times why you do them? The reason is that it gives you a false sense of being in control. In reality, these activities do not give people control at all. In reality, these things *control them.*

When you overeat, you end up having heart problems- or you end up having other health issues, such as diabetes. We are not speaking about people with thyroid issues here.

We are talking about those of us who eat more than we should for comfort!

When you drink too much alcohol, you can get liver disease and other related problems. You may have trouble staying gainfully employed and alcohol abuse often leads to relationship issues and costly DUIs.

When you do illegal drugs, it ruins your health. Heroin users often overdose and die-or use a tainted batch and go into cardiac arrest. Meth users become paranoid, fail to eat healthily and lose their teeth. Heavy marijuana users end up losing the motivation to do anything other than to get high. Use of the drug often causes them to be unable to keep a job or to have meaningful relationships. Oxycodone users can end up losing their hearing. Use of any illegal drug can often lead to financial ruin. You get the picture.

So why do we think these things can give us control?

Well, the reality is that control can only be had in a true and meaningful way, as we submit to, and yield ourselves entirely to the God Who made us!

From the very beginning, God created us to live for Him.

So how in the world did things get so messed up?

Let's go back to the beginning. In the very beginning, when God created Adam and Eve, the first two people who ever lived, the parents of the human race- He didn't give them a bunch of rules.

He gave them only one rule.

He put them in a beautiful paradise, called the Garden of Eden in the Holy Bible. And in that garden, among all of the most beautiful plants, trees, flowers, and animals that ever existed-there were two very prominent trees.

They were the "tree of life" AND the "tree of the knowledge of good and evil."

In addition to God telling man to take care of the garden (work was originally a good thing-and still can be today), and giving Adam the job of naming all of the animals, God also told Adam, "Of every tree of the garden you may freely eat [you can have any of it]; but of the tree of the knowledge of good and evil you shall not eat, for in the day that you eat of it you shall surely die[i]."

The consequence, or the result, of Adam eating from that tree would be death- spiritual and physical death both for himself and for the entire human race.

That was the one command that he had to obey.

Later God would give other commandments as they became necessary[ii]. But in the very beginning, there was just one commandment. Several thousand years later Jesus summed up obedience to God in two commandments.

When asked by a religious leader what the most important commandment was, Jesus answered him, "The first of all the commandments *is:* 'Hear, O Israel, the LORD our God, the LORD is one. And you shall love the LORD your God with all your heart, with all your soul, with all your mind, and with all your strength.' This *is* the first commandment. And the second, like *it, is* this: 'You shall love your neighbor as yourself.' There is no other commandment greater than these[iii]."

FALSE CONTROL-REAL CONTROL

You see, God made us with the purpose of having our lives controlled by a relationship of loving obedience to Him. We know that this is true from what is popularly called today, the Lord's Prayer. When Jesus' closest followers asked him, "Lord, teach us to pray?" He taught them this prayer:

> Our Father, who art in heaven, hallowed be thy name. Thy kingdom come, thy will be done on earth as it is in heaven. Give us this day our daily bread, and forgive us our trespasses as we forgive those who trespass against us. And lead us not into temptation, but deliver us from the evil one[iv].

In this prayer, Jesus teaches us to pray to God, "Thy kingdom come, thy will be done on earth, as it is in heaven." When Adam and Eve disobeyed God they essentially said, "My kingdom come, my will be done."

When Eve was tricked, or deceived, by the serpent, she disobeyed the command of God and she gave some of the fruit to her husband, Adam who willingly disobeyed the command of God and ate it[v]. This was the beginning of the earthly creation becoming subjected to sin and death. The world was taken over by the devil.

You see, sin is disobeying God and His commands.

Righteousness, on the other hand, is obedience to God-this is also called "holiness."

So the world was created very good from the beginning. It says in Genesis-the first book of the Bible- "Then God saw everything that He had made, and indeed it was very good[vi]." That's what it says. God didn't make it bad. He didn't create evil[vii].

But there was an old deceiver, called the devil, the serpent of old, the dragon, Satan[viii], who had rebelled against God. He had disobeyed God and said, "I will be like the Most High[ix]." And because of his jealousy of mankind who had been made in the image and likeness of God[x], the devil in the form of a snake came, tempted, and ultimately deceived our first mother, Eve.

That serpent of old, the enemy of our souls, was seeking to disrupt the fellowship of human beings with God. And as we see from the Bible and history, sadly, he was very successful. But the devil was not the ultimate victor.

The ultimate Victor was and is the **Lord Jesus Christ**[xi], who by his complete obedience to the will of God, in our place as a human being (yet fully God) defeated sin, death, and the devil for us. The Son of God in the flesh obeyed God even to the point of death, even death on the cross, as it says in Philippians 2[xii].

JESUS reconciled us to God[xiii].

Paul, the Apostle talks about Adam, and he speaks of Jesus as the last Adam[xiv]. Everything that Adam was supposed to be - a human being in complete submission to the perfect will of God-Jesus became, for us. As Christians, He is our wisdom and righteousness and sanctification[xv].

So how does all of this relate to control?

God, from the beginning, created human beings to have closeness with him, to have a relationship with him and ruling this world as His representatives.

How does my son relate to me if he's in a good relationship with me? He says, “Yes, Papa” and he does what I ask him to do. And we have a great relationship because I'm his father, and he's my son, and I love him.

Now, in today's world with all of the rebellious children and with all of the rebellious parents this is not something that always makes sense to us. But, we do see from the example of history and the teaching of the Bible, that parents are to be obeyed[xvi].

Children are to obey their parents. Paul says this in the New Testament, “Children, obey your parents in the Lord, for this is right[xvii].” By the way, he also says, “And you, fathers, do not provoke your children to wrath, but bring them up in the training and admonition of the Lord[xviii].”

You see, God created us to have a relationship with Him as His children. When Adam and Eve disobeyed God, they decided to listen to another voice. They did not obey God's voice. They listened to the voice of the evil one. To the voice of the murderer who is from the beginning[xix], the devil.

When we obey God, by faith in Jesus Christ, His only begotten Son, we are submitting our lives to God and living out the prayer that Jesus taught us to pray; "Your kingdom come, Your will be done, on earth, as it is in heaven[xx]."

What is "Kingdom?"

Kingdom is rulership.

It is God's rulership in our lives.

This is the reason why when you see a real Christian who has the Holy Spirit working in their life-you see that he or she consistently does what is pleasing to God. His or her life is characterized by doing only things that are acceptable to God. We're not talking about rules. What we're talking about is a good child who loves his or her father and seeks only to please his or her dad.

So, control, how do you get it? You let go of it…

-You don't try to get it through overeating.

-You don't try to get it by manipulating people through being passive-aggressive or by deception.

-You don’t get it through using pornography or through sexual addiction.

-You don't get it by trying to be powerful and trying to be famous and trying to be in charge of others.

-You don’t get it through gambling away your paycheck.

-You don’t get it through worrying about all of your problems all of the time until it makes your stomach hurt or gives you a headache, or paralyzes you with fear.

++You get it by allowing the Holy Spirit of God to *control* your life.

Paul, the Apostle says to the Christians in the ancient city of Corinth, "Do you not know that you [all] are the temple of God and that the Spirit of God dwells in you[xxi]?" God Himself, lives inside the true Christian, controlling his or her life and giving them the power to yield themselves entirely to God. You can have a life of control by fully allowing God to have control of your life- your thoughts, your words, your heart, your actions, even your attitudes, and your emotions.

Do you feel out of control in your emotions?
Let God have control of your heart and your mind.

Do you feel out of control in the decisions you've been making lately?

Read the Bible and see what God has to say about those decisions. Pray and ask the Holy Spirit to make clear to you what is right and wrong and what you should do.

Do you feel socially isolated? Go to a Christian church that teaches the Bible.

Allow God to have control of your life in every area and aspect: In your personal life, in what you do with your free time. In your family life-in what you do with those closest to you. In what you do in your social life.

Allow God to have control of these things. Allow God to have control of the things that you say. That you don't gossip. That you don't slander other people[xxii]. That you don't make fun of other people. That you say kind words[xxiii]. That you say helpful things[xxiv]. That you say thoughtful things.

Maybe you're chronically overweight; this is the solution for you. Allow the God and Father of the Lord Jesus Christ, by the power and presence of the Holy Spirit, to have dominion, to have "kingdom," to have rulership over your life in this area and in all areas. Eat healthy things in moderation. Eat portions that are thought out. Don't eat until you're stuffed and then eat some more. Don't even always eat until you're full. Eat the daily bread that you need. Like Jesus, taught us to pray, "Give us this day our daily bread."

Maybe you have a problem with smoking. Perhaps you're a chain smoker, and you smoke a lot. You're likely going to get lung cancer like my grandmother who died from that unless you quit. If you can allow God to have control in your life, He will set you free (even from that which is more addictive than the drug of heroin).

Maybe you're an angry person; you believe that being angry puts you in control. It doesn't. Being angry can give you ulcers, it can give you a stroke and can lead to violent confrontations with other people- or even to a heart attack. Have you ever realized that you don't have any more control when you get really angry than before you lost your temper? Getting mad gives you a false sense of control.

So you see in this clear teaching, that all sin ultimately comes from not allowing God to have control in your life[xxv].

God has control in our lives when we allow Him to- when we pray and do the things that He has said. When you obey what He says in His Word (the Bible) you will have life. The most important thing that He says is "Believe on the Lord Jesus Christ, and you will be saved, you and your household" (Acts 16:31).

God is the Lord, which means that God is the King[xxvi]. "Lord" means King, Master, or Ruler. God is the true Ruler of the entire universe, not the devil who tried to take control.

That's what the snake was trying to do. The devil was trying to take dominion (rulership) from mankind. When he could not gain control of the whole universe after attempting to take God's place, the devil tried to take man's place, by taking control of the created world.

Since God had given mankind dominion over the fish of the sea and over the birds of the air and over every creature[xxvii], we know that God originally put man in charge of this world, as His representative. God gave mankind the authority over this world. And so when the devil successfully tempted man, he was able to take control for a time.

After 40 days of fasting in the wilderness, the devil came and tempted Jesus. The Bible records, "Again, the devil took Him [Jesus] up on an exceedingly high mountain, and showed Him all the kingdoms of the world and their glory. And he said to Him, 'All these things I will give You if You will fall down and worship me[xxviii].'"

The kingdoms of the world were, in fact, the devil's to give because he had gotten dominion from the man when Adam chose to disobey God and instead to obey the devil.

The Good News is that Jesus redeemed it all back by His death upon the cross[xxix]. And one day He'll return to claim it all back and will make all things right when He appears in His glory with all of His holy angels[xxx].

When we by faith in Jesus Christ allow God full control of our lives we escape the control of the devil and are delivered from the power of our fleshly nature. We become free from the false sense of control that we feel through wrong and unhelpful behaviors (sin). We let go of control and allow the One Who made us to have the proper place which He designed for our lives. When we let go of control we ask God to control us. Then and only then, are we able to have real control- self-control by the work of God in our lives[xxxi].

God bless you and thank you for reading this book.

About the Author

PASTOR JASON TERPACK is an Author, Husband, Father, and Minister. He is a decorated War Veteran of the United States Air Force and loves to help people. Jason and his family make their home in Southern California.

NOTES

---

[i] Genesis 2:16-17

[ii] See Exodus chapter 20

[iii] Mark 12:29-31

[iv] Popular version of the prayer found in Matthew 6:9-13

[v] Genesis chapter 3

[vi] Genesis 1:31

[vii] 1 Corinthians 14:33

[viii] Revelation 20:2

[ix] Isaiah 14:14

[x] Genesis 1:26-27

[xi] 1 Corinthians 15:57

[xii] Philippians 2:5-11

[xiii] Colossians 1:19-20

[xiv] 1 Corinthians chapter 15

[xv] 1 Corinthians 1:30

[xvi] Exodus 20:12

[xvii] Ephesians 6:1

[xviii] Ephesians 6:4

[xix] John 8:44

[xx] Matthew 6:10

[xxi] 1 Corinthians 3:16

[xxii] Colossians 3:8

[xxiii] 1 Thessalonians 5:11

[xxiv] Ephesians 4:29

[xxv] Other examples of sins where one attempts to feel in control include: self-harm, compulsive shopping, chauvinism, feminism, racism, etc.

[xxvi] Deuteronomy 10:17, Psalm 136:3, 1 Timothy 6:15, Revelation 19:16

[xxvii] Genesis 1:28

[xxviii] Matthew 4:8-9

[xxix] 1 Peter 1:18-25

[xxx] Matthew 25:21-46

[xxxi] Galatians 5:22-23

www.ingramcontent.com/pod-product-compliance
Ingram Content Group UK Ltd.
Pitfield, Milton Keynes, MK11 3LW, UK
UKHW041901190726
13854UKWH00003B/1013